MAN! KNOW THYSELF

Being a talk given by

SANT KIRPAL SINGH JI

For seekers after Truth

Kind hearts are the gardens,
Kind thoughts are the roots;
Kind words are the blossoms,
Kind deeds are the fruits.

TABLE OF CONTENTS

RUHANI SATSANG®
Divine Science of the Soul
250 "H" Street, #50
Blaine, WA 98230-4033

First Published: January 1954
Twentieth Printing: October 2005

Printed in the United States of America
By Print Graphics Pros • (949) 859-3845

Sant Kirpal Singh Ji
(1894-1974)

About the Author:

Considered by many people who met him in the East and in the West to have been a living example of a true Saint of spirituality, Kirpal Singh was born in a rural setting in Sayyad Kasran in the Punjab (then in India, now in Pakistan) on February 6, 1894. He followed the career of a civil servant in the government of India, and retired on his own pension in 1947. Following instructions from his Master (Sawan Singh Ji Maharaj, 1858-1948), he founded and directed RUHANI SATSANG. He was Commissioned by God and authorized by his Master to carry forward the spiritual work of contacting sincere seekers after God with the WORD (or NAAM). He continued in that capacity until he left the earth plane on August 21, 1974. Elected four times, consecutively, as President of the World Fellowship of Religions, he upheld the truth that, though the various religions are different schools of thought, the Aim of all religions is One and the Same. Kirpal Singh visited the major cities in the United States on the occasions of each of his three world tours: in 1955, in 1963-64, and again in 1972, staying in this country for three months or more, each time. From his intense study at the feet of Sawan Singh Ji Maharaj and from his own personal inner experiences of a spiritual nature, Kirpal Singh was eminently qualified to convey to sincere people everywhere the importance of self knowledge and God realization.

Foreword

THE NEED OF spiritual science or Science of the Soul has ever been felt by man through the ages. Its need today is as great as ever before; perhaps greater. By a ceaseless effort of centuries, man has no doubt succeeded to a great extent to control the forces of Nature and to press them into his service. But unfortunately, as this control has come to him before gaining Self-Knowledge—knowing one's Self and one's relation to humanity—all his discoveries and inventions, originally intended and designed for the service of mankind, are being turned into instruments of destruction and devastation. With all his inner craving for peace and his professions and protestations in this behalf, he has failed to serve his cause. His ideology of peace apart, he, through lack of Self-Knowledge, is unwittingly sowing the seeds of class hatred, racial discrimination, national passions and prejudices, and international discord and disruption. The peace of the world, for want of proper understanding, hangs today by a very slender thread. The social injustices and economic inequalities rampant everywhere have made people skeptical of God and distrustful of each other. Cut off from their very moorings, they drift rudderless along the stream of life and look askance and bewildered. The armed peace, the perpetual fear and inherent helplessness in which we live, is not an ideal state to be desired. We want instead a living peace, based on fraternal love and good will, mutual trust and respect for each other as children of the same Supreme Father.

The idea of real and lasting inner peace is not a mere ideology, but can be turned into an actual reality if one could but introvert and peep within, know his real Self or soul, and arise in Cosmic Awareness. This can be achieved only through close contact with some Godman or Mastersoul—call him what you will—an Adept well-versed not only in the theory but also in the practice of Para Vidya or the Science of the Soul.

With this end in view, the beloved Master originally gave this thought provoking talk—MAN! KNOW THYSELF—for listeners abroad. It has now been put into print for the benefit of all persons who are seekers after Truth, irrespective of caste, color or creed. If it inspires even a single soul with a longing for Self-Knowledge and God-Knowledge, the efforts of the Ruhani Satsang will be amply rewarded.

Delhi, January 17, 1954 BHADRA SENA

Man! Know Thyself

SINCE THE BEGINNING of Creation, when the first flicker of self-awakening dawned on man, his attention has been more and more concerned with the problem of his own worldly existence and the investigation into the cause and source of all Creation. For ages he has probed and queried in vain; but now at last his increasing thirst for knowledge is turning him to study the results achieved by others in the field.

Ancient and modern sages asked, "What is that, the knowledge of which makes everything else known?" and in the same breath replied, "Knowledge of the Higher Self—the True Man." So the Supreme Knowledge is that which deals, both in theory and practice, with Man's true nature and his relation to God. It is in fact a natural science without hypothesis, subject neither to change nor time.

In ancient India it was called "Para Vidya" (Science of Realized Truth or Science of the Beyond), and different denominations sprang up to interpret this knowledge. The term "Apra Vidya," standing for preparation for achieving the knowledge of Para Vidya, was then introduced. This preparation consists of following an ethical and moral life, and the practice of concentration or meditation (in so many ways), both being indispensable for spiritual development.

Man is constantly changing or introducing new names and terminologies to describe this Science. The Masters were called "Sant," and the nature of knowledge "Mat," thus giving us the term "Sant Mat," which is at present mostly used to name the Path of the Masters. Other terms, such as Shabd Yoga, Surat Shabd Yoga, Sehaj Yoga, are also used to describe the same

Science. In the Sanskrit language, the word "Sant" means a Master of the Highest Order; and "Mat" is a confirmed opinion or statement made by an adept after personal experience. The foundation of this Science therefore is the result of critical study, minute investigation, and the life-long personal verification of facts based on practical experience of the Self in man. This experience of the Self is something that a competent Master is prepared to give to each individual who approaches him. Sant Mat, therefore, is the teaching, system, and path of the Saints.

The Masters do not attach any importance to names, designations, or the fact that many religious sects, groups and circles have claimed this Science as their own and named it after their leaders or founders. They look upon these groups as schools where man—the noblest being in Creation—can study with other men as children of one and the same Almighty Father. A Master (also called Sant Satguru) has complete mastery of both theory and practice, and is competent to impart both knowledge and experience to all sincere seekers after Truth, without any distinction whatever of color, caste or creed. Any man or woman, whether rich or poor, young or old, sage or sinner, learned or unlearned, who is able to grasp the theory of the Science has a right to acquire this knowledge.

Present Fate of Various Beliefs and Faiths

The dictionary defines "mat" as wisdom; but the colloquial meaning of the term is a sect or faith, a group of people holding certain opinions or beliefs in common. Such beliefs and opinions, however, based on stray knowledge and teachings, are not sufficient without the support of personal experience; and therefore the seeker is led astray by mere empty words. Many societies, faiths, and other religious circles have only a legacy of books, beliefs and theories to offer to those who thirst after Spirituality. They conceal their shortcomings and deficiencies behind a screen of warm welcome, an outpouring of technique and terminology, and the liberal use of sayings and quotations from the enormous mass of literature on the market today. Propaganda and acting and posing have taken the place of practical Spirituality, with the result that the deluded public is being repelled from sacred books and thoughts of God. Atheism therefore is on the increase.

To believe in a thing or fact without troubling to investigate it does not in any way do credit to an intelligent man. On the contrary, it reflects adversely on his ignorance or credulity. Any belief not based on personal experience and verification of the facts has little value. The modern man wants a well-defined, clear cut Science, capable of verification by his own experience and giving concrete results. We should therefore try to see and to hear with our own eyes and ears rather than with the eyes and ears of others.

Self-Analysis

Man is composed of body, mind (intellect) and soul. We are extremely careful to develop ourselves physically and mentally, but understand very little about the soul, which is the power ruling both the body and the mind. Physical joys are not lasting, and there are limitations of body and mind that we cannot ignore; so we must search for the perennial source of joy and peace within ourselves. Self-analysis is the first step in this direction.

Many doubts assail our minds at this stage. There is an Omnipotent Power called God, believed in, worshiped and talked about by most people. Can we know more about Him? Can we see Him and talk to Him? There is a definite and clear reply to these questions; the Master in a few brief words explains, "Yes, we can see and speak to Him; that is, if we become as exalted as He is said to be." Masters say "Yes," and we do not have to wait until death comes, but we can experience it right now. This is in consonance with Laws of Nature of which we have as yet no knowledge worth the name.

All around us we see and feel that everything from the tiny atom to the mighty Universe is governed by a Law of Nature. So, to the profound thinker, there is nothing chaotic, haphazard or uncertain about this Universe and the laws which govern it. To gain any objective, there is a Law of Nature, a principle and method involved for checking, testing and weighing the result of our endeavors. So it is too in this Science of Nature, and similar methods can be traced in all religious scriptures by any careful student, though expressed in different words and various languages.

We wish to enter the Kingdom of God, but how? we ask ourselves. "With the help and guidance of one who has himself entered and can guide us there," is the simple reply from the Masters. "Is it possible?" "It is a knowledge which is as exact and sure as two and two make four," is again their reply. It is not enough to be content with holy books and the singing of praises and hymns. We must strive for the same degree of advancement as the authors of the talks and knowledge recorded in these books achieved. Their experience must become our experience, for "what a man has done, a man can do"; of course, with proper help and guidance. We should stop at nothing short of this.

"We have hardly a dim spark of love for Him; will it help to cherish a hope?" is another question asked, to which the Saints reply, "It is sufficient to make you eligible for the Highest Science of approach to Him." This is a pleasing ray of hope. Oh! if this small spark could be kindled into a flame! Again, we say, "Jesus and other great Masters spoke so lovingly of Him, but we are sinners and there may not be much hope for us in this age." The Masters' soothing reply is, "No matter if you are the worst of sinners, stop where you are. There is hope for everybody, even in this crucial age." Ages ago, Nature provided for us materially and spiritually. Today the same unchangeable Law is operating and will continue to do so in the future. There is food for the hungry and water for the thirsty. Nature's inexorable and eternal Law of demand and supply always works.

It is only through a living Master that we can contact the Almighty God within us. In Sant Mat, contemplation of objects or images is not advised, as this is harmful to progress. Photographs of the Masters are for remembrance and recognition only, and on no account should we become attached to such external practices.

The Teachings of the Masters (Man-Making)

A man, according to the science of Para Vidya, is not entitled to be called a man in the true sense of the word unless he has full knowledge, both theoretical and practical, of his distinguished position in Creation, his several component parts—body, mind, and soul—in order of comparative importance, and of his relationship to the Unseen Power called God; which is to be achieved while he is living on this earth. He who does not understand this much has not even been introduced to the first lesson and is yet to begin the Alphabet of Man. The Saints therefore impress upon us the need for "Man-making."

Satsang

When scientifically observed facts drawn from practice and experiment are explained verbally to a gathering by a Master Saint, it is called Satsang (external). This Satsang constitutes the theoretical side of the teachings; whereas the actual demonstration given to develop and achieve inner advancement is the practical part, called meditation or Satsang (internal). Conscientious practice brings fruit within days or weeks and it is not necessary to wait years for results, though progress also depends to some extent on one's past background. A true Master gives a first-hand inner experience at the very first sitting. When the practical side is neglected due to lack of firmness or determination, carelessness or pressure of circumstances, scholars of many religious schools dwell more and more upon theory alone. The decline of the Science then commences and man finds no solace. This is usually the case when a Master leaves the body. Adequate provision however is made for the revival of this Science in every age, when both the Positive and Negative Powers commence their rounds again: the former through the agency of Master-souls, while the latter works through persons—so-called Masters—who lack practical experience or are lost in theoretical disputations. Master-souls, though quite ordinary men in appearance, are a great deal more. Just as it is difficult for us to judge a scientist, a doctor or an engineer until they speak out or display their skill and knowledge, so too we cannot recognize the knowledge and authority of a Master until we have experienced the Divine Power working through him.

In this Science there is no secrecy or mystery. The objective is constructive and beneficial to all, and so the Saints have torn aside the curtain of secrecy which usually covers mystic teachings to make them available to each and every one who calls. There is an Unseen Power working through the Saints. Why this Power prefers to remain concealed from the human eye is a question to be asked directly by contacting the human pole through whom this Power is working. This is the only medium of approach to this Power. If we wish to use electric energy we must go to a switch or pole which will put us in contact with the powerhouse. The Unseen Power may be called a Sea of Love. When we wish to bathe in the sea, we go to the edge where the shallow waters begin and then say that we have bathed in the sea. Thus, to experience this Power and to derive benefit from it, we must go to the only source of contact—a Master Saint.

Life Beyond Death

Saints say that Nature has designed man to leave his physical body at will, transcend to higher spiritual planes, and then return to the body. They help each aspirant personally and each receives a practical experience, however little it may be, during the very first sitting at the time of Initiation. A person who is competent to give a man this personal experience of withdrawal or separation (temporary) from the body, and who can thus put him on the way back to God, is a genuine Master, Saint, or Satguru. The heads of different religious organizations were intended to do just this, but we may judge for ourselves their efficacy today.

The first-hand experience we receive, through the kindness of a real Saint, is in itself the solution to the problem of death. According to the Bible, "Unless you are born anew, you cannot enter into the Kingdom of God." So to be born anew is to leave one's body and enter into the Beyond—a transition from the physical to the astral plane. Some day we have to leave this temporary structure, which like a building of bricks and mortar deteriorates with time. There is no appeal to the Laws of Nature against the "death sentence." We fear death because of the agony and suffering which it brings, and also because of the uncertainty that lies ahead in the Beyond. We fear illness because it brings us near death's door; so we struggle to live though we know that our end is certain. No soothing words from doctors, friends, relatives or priests can bring peace and comfort to our minds at the time that Nature's destructive process commences. This is the natural course of things and we cannot deceive Nature.

What then is the remedy? There is only one way out of this abyss of despair: to adopt and accustom ourselves, during our lifetime, to Nature's process of the withdrawal of the spirit current from the body, while still in a conscious state. This may be done with the help of a Master, and may be accomplished without any suffering or trouble whatever. This is not only a possibility but is a remarkable fact. Our joy will know no bounds when we come into possession of the secret that has baffled man for so many centuries. We become supermen, having possession of a key to peace and heaven, the life of which we had till then only read about in sacred scriptures. Arise, therefore, and awake! before it is too late to put this Science into practice. If we observe closely the process of death in a dying man, we see the pupils of his eyes turn upwards a little (afterwards they may return to normal) and then he becomes senseless. But when they draw upwards too much, he dies. Life ebbs out via the root of the eyes and becomes disconnected from the ties of the physical body and the sense organs. Knowledge of this process and the method by which we may travel this Way during our very lifetime is the solution to the problem of death. No physical exercises are necessary; there are no drugs to swallow and no blind faith to cultivate. The mystery of life and death is solved easily with the help of a Master Saint, who will give you an experience of the process and put you on the highway to the inner realms. Even when acting indirectly through an authorized agent, he still remains the responsible power. Distance is immaterial to the Masters.

What is there to be gained by this process? This cannot be described in words. At the time of Initiation, the aspirant sees the real Light within him, whereas normally the inner eye is covered by a thick veil of darkness. He then realizes that the tradition of the lighted candle found in churches and temples is to remind him of the Divine Light of Heaven within. This Light grows to the radiance of several suns put together as he advances on the Way. He understands that the unceasing internal Sound he contacts within is the Divine Link called "Word" by Christ, "Kalma" and "Nida-i-Asmani" in the Koran, "Nad" in the Vedas, "Udgit" in the Upanishads, "Sarosha" by the Zoroastrians, and "Naam" and "Shabd" by the Saints and Masters. In time, he meets the Master within, talks to him face to face, and is henceforth certain of his grace, guidance and protection wherever he may go, even to the other end of the world. With such evident proofs before him, he is now confident of himself and of the Science. Only then can he be called a theist in the true sense of the word, and can smile at those who talk of religion as a fool's paradise, a phantom conjured up by crafty priests, and the opium of the masses. He has found a sure ingress through the doorway of heaven in this life, and is on the threshold of viewing, both internally and externally, the secrets of Nature. He is truly "knocking at the door of Heaven" or "tapping inside." Words of opposition cannot shake his faith in the Science as the Master guides him onward. Death becomes a voluntary process. Past, present and future merge into one, and he grasps the incontestable Truth, the essence of Being, in the palm of his hand. Liberated from the body, which now appears as a husk without the kernel, he knows that he is Soul, an inseparable part of the Eternal Spirit, and so he presses onward to his original source. The world appears as a dream to him, but under the instructions from his Master, he returns to his mundane life, wise and fearless in the discharge of his duties.

Preliminary Qualifications for an Aspirant on the Way

Just as in any other science, certain preliminary qualifications are required before much progress can be made. Married life, hard work, or a poor environment are no bar. It does not count in your favor that you may hold a high position or possess immense wealth. Neither does membership in a particular faith serve as a recommendation. Wherever he may be, a man must strive for nobility of character, self-control and purity of heart. Purity of heart in thought, word, and deed, is essential. "Blessed are the pure in heart for they shall see God." An ethical life is a stepping stone to Spirituality, but Spirituality is however not just ethical living. This we must always bear in mind.

We can divide man's life into (i) diet, and (ii) his dealings with others. With regard to diet, vegetarianism and abstinence from alcohol and drugs are essential. "Thou shalt not kill" and "Live and let live" should be our principles in life. The body is the temple of God and is a sacred place. We are not to neglect or abuse it, but should take the best possible care to properly maintain it. All intoxicants are also to be avoided as they make us morbid and of shaky consciousness. With regard to our dealings with others, we should sow the seed of kindness in order to reap its fruit. Love and humility are most necessary. "Do unto others as you would have them do unto you." "Love, and all blessings shall be added unto you." "Love thine enemy, and do good to them that despitefully use you." God is immanent in every form and whoever loves God, must love God's Creation. To love God is to love all humanity. We should also earn our living by the sweat of our brow and share with others. These are not empty sayings, but very wise and sound advice.

Karma (Actions and Deeds)

Each thought, each word and each deed has to be accounted for and compensated for in Nature. Every cause has an effect and every action brings about a reaction. Uproot the cause and the effect disappears. This has been done by the Masters who have transcended these laws, but all others are bound by the bonds of Karma, which is the root cause of physical existence and the clever device of Nature to maintain this existence. The law of Karma sees to it that we are paid an eye for an eye and tooth for a tooth, in the shape of joy or suffering. It is the goading whip in the hidden hands of Nature. The mind contracts Karma, puts a covering on the soul and rules the body through the organs and the senses. Although it is the soul that imparts strength to the mind, the latter has assumed sovereignty and is governing the soul instead. Control of the mind, therefore, is the first step to Spirituality. Victory over the mind is victory over the world. Even accomplished yogis and mystics who can transcend to relatively high spiritual realms are not left untouched by the hand of Karma.

Saints classify Karmas into three distinct groups, as follows:

(i) **Sanchit** (stored): Good or bad deeds that stand to our account as earned and contracted in all previous bodies of the order of Creation, counting from the day of the first appearance of life on earth. Alas! Man knows nothing about them or their extent.

(ii) **Prarabdha** (Fate or Destiny): The result and effect of which has brought man into his present body and has to be paid off in this life. The reactions of these Karmas come to us unexpectedly and unperceived and we have no control over them whatsoever. Good or bad, we have to tolerate or bear this Karma laughing or weeping, as it happens to suit us.

(iii) **Kriyaman** (Account of our actions and deeds in the present body): This is distinct from the above mentioned two groups because here man is free to do exactly as he pleases, within certain limits. Knowingly or unknowingly, deeds committed and coming under this heading bear fruit. The result of some of these we reap before we die and the residue is transferred to the Sanchit storehouse.

Karma is the cause of rebirth and each birth is in turn followed by death. Thus the cycle of enjoyment and suffering, which are concomitants of birth and death, continues. "As you think, so you become," is an unalterable Law of Nature, owing to which this Universe exists. No amount of integrity or genius can absolve a man so long as there is the slightest trace of Karma. Ignorance of the Law is no excuse, and though there may be some concession or relaxation with man-made laws under special circumstances, there is no such allowance made for this in Nature's Laws. Prayer, confession and atonement may give temporary mental relief but they cannot overcome Karma. All Karma must be wiped out completely before permanent salvation can be had.

Disturbed by these facts, Man seeks solace in deep pious doctrines, or when he comes to know that both good and bad deeds are fetters—one of gold, the other of iron—he turns to Renunciation. Different faiths promise relief but he soon finds out that this is only temporary. How then does a Master approach this problem? At the time of Initiation, the Master begins the process of winding up all Karmas of the initiate. He gives him a contact with the Sound Current, by practicing which the Sanchit account is burnt away. The process is similar to putting a handful of seeds in a pan and placing them on a fire, which then causes the seeds to puff up and lose their property of growing again. Then the Kriyaman account is dealt with. After warning his disciples to guard against opening any new account of bad deeds, the Master grants a general clemency in respect of bad deeds, part of which the disciple has already settled in this life up to the time of Initiation. He is enjoined to lead a clean life and to weed out all imperfections in him by self-introspection from day to day. The Prarabdha Karma is not touched by Saints because this is the cause of the physical body, which would vanish due to the interference with Nature's Laws. Thus a very small amount of Karma now remains to be tolerated in the physical body for the remaining years of the disciple's life, but even this is softened by the grace of the Master. The law of grace works wonders and a devotee who, out of loving devotion, reposes all his hopes in the Master, passes off unscathed from the pinching effects of the reactions of past Karmas. In moments of misery, worry and trouble, the Master is our refuge. He acts unperceived at any distance. Just as a mother of a sick child holds the child securely in her lap during an operation so that it does not feel any pain, so too the Master holds us in his loving embrace. Out of their abundance of sympathy, love and kindness, the Saints at times take upon their own shoulders some Karmic sufferings of their disciples through the Law of Sympathy. There is no court of trial after death for a devoted disciple. The Master is all in all for him.

Why does a Master Saint take all this on himself? Because he inherits his merciful nature from God above, who commissions him to personally distribute this treasure of mercy. Thus the Master is honored like God. Sant Mat has volumes of books written in praise of the Masters, and if just as many books were to be written, it would hardly do justice to the vastness of their love and kindness.

Time casts its heavy shadow over man. He has to work hard to keep pace with the changing times. So deeply is he absorbed in his external needs and desires that he forgets all about contentment, sympathy and love. Entangled and surrounded by the "Deadly Five"—lust, anger, greed, attachment and vanity—he stumbles and cries out to the Unseen for help. Heaven's mercy is stirred and as times stiffen, the Almighty extends His help through the Masters more and more lavishly. Such is the case in this Kali Yuga—the Iron Age.

It is indeed very hard to believe that anyone can be above the five passions mentioned above, and that he can enter the Kingdom of Heaven during his lifetime. All mankind is under the control of these five and only a Master can save a man from their clutches. We all demand reliable proof before committing ourselves, and this is given by a Master in the shape of an experience of the life impulse or Naam (the Word) and some inner vision. Contact with a Master is essential. Those who keep aloof and depend on themselves or rely on tradition and priests—equally ignorant as themselves—are deprived of contact with this Power; and as the saying goes, "When the blind lead the blind, both fall into the ditch."

Indifference, non-acceptance or disbelief will not be to our advantage when Nature enforces its Universal Ordinance—Death. Our position will be that of a pigeon who, on seeing a cat approaching, shuts its eyes and believes that the cat cannot then molest it; but in a few seconds the poor bird is in the powerful jaws of the cat. It is then too late to think of escape. So be alert while there is yet time!

Spirituality

Perhaps it will not be out of place to explain here the meaning of the term "Spirituality," which is often confused with blind faith in sacred books, a display of miracles, psychic phenomena, or Yogic powers. Spirituality is an inner experience and its alphabet begins where all philosophy and Yoga practices end. It is the experience of the soul. When one says, "I am the body," it is a feeling based on the intellect and is defined as ignorance. When he says, "I am not the body, I am an awakened soul," it is learnt knowledge or theory only; but when he gets an actual experience of the soul by self-analysis and contacts the Overself, it is called Spirituality. The first practical lesson commences when there is a complete withdrawal from the physical body through the kindness of a practical Master. No one can withdraw and separate himself from the physical body unaided. If anyone claims otherwise and thinks that he can, he but deceives himself. All attempts without the assistance of a Master, who alone is qualified to impart this experience, will end in failure. Masters come to distribute this treasure of spiritual blessings to seekers after Truth. Spirituality cannot be bought or taught, but it can be caught by contact with spiritual people. Moreover, Nature's gifts such as air, water, light, etc., are free. Spirituality is also Nature's gift and is also given free by the Masters. Likewise, Spirituality cannot be acquired from books, which is a fact all sacred scriptures uphold. Books are a valuable record of the inner experiences of others in Spirituality. They fill up gaps in history and contain messages from past Masters, which help us to verify the facts revealed by a living Master, thus confirming our faith in the Science. Man is confused by the various translations, interpretations and expositions, each different from the other, which instead of relieving his mind, tend rather to bewilder and confuse him. His egoism too has created hundreds of religious circles, whose aim is aloofness and narrow orthodoxy instead of love, and insularity instead of integration. Torn between conflicting emotions, men develop hatred and think of war.

For an understanding of the Science of the Masters, we attend Satsang, where the majority of our doubts are cleared. Direct answers from the Master will help to remove any remaining doubts. All questions receive the same calm consideration and no arguments are offered. Rich or poor, high or low, all receive equal attention in the same manner as a doctor should attend to the sick. A true Master views a man's rights and wrongs as clearly as one sees the contents of a glass jar, but he reveals nothing. Sitting before him, even those who do not understand his language are benefited, just as one in a perfumer's shop enjoys the smell of sweet scents. The Master showers blessings through his looks, which the eager ones catch. His eyes are a wonderful spray of love.

The Criterion for Judging a Genuine Master

Do not judge a Master by his external appearance, genealogical descent, rich or poor attire, country of origin, how he talks, eats or the position he holds, the number of books that he is the author of, or by what people say about him. First receive the inner experience he promises; then judge from that elevated angle of vision. Self-experience is the criterion for judging a genuine Master. Any living person who sees things from a spiritual level—man and his embarrassments, difficulties and helplessness—and who has studied the problems confronting humanity, can provide their solutions, and is also able to correct and guide man visibly and invisibly, morally and spiritually, in theory as well as in practice. Only such a person is fit to take the responsible position of a Master. Blessed are those who experience a stirring emotion of happiness and longing in their hearts on hearing the news that such a Master exists and is near.

Spirituality is a science simpler and easier than other sciences. Man has not to exert except in molding himself ethically and morally to the climax of love, sincerity and humility, which will produce the necessary state of receptivity in him. Everything else is in the hands of the Master. Again, a movement, no matter how spiritual it may appear to be on the surface, should not be judged by the number of followers that it has. A good speaker can attract crowds anywhere, yet there may not be anything material or convincing in his speech. Spirituality is not the exclusive possession of any family or place, but it is like a scented flower that grows wherever Nature has ordained, around which the bees gather from far and wide to sip its nectar. Masters do not rush after glory of self, although they certainly deserve such glory. Even in ordinary talks, they will be heard to say, "Oh, it is all the grace of my Master. It is none of my doing. My Master deserves all the praise and credit." This humility places them far above the low level of egoism found in this world.

Masters have come in all ages to offer this Natural Science to man. Only those who are discontented with this world rush to them. Others, to whom worldly attractions, pleasures and luxuries are dear, turn their backs. Those in whose hearts all noble sentiments are dead not only put all possible obstacles in the way of the Saints, but also subject them to various kinds of tortures, as a study of the lives of Jesus, Guru Nanak, Kabir and others will show. Masters have come in the past, are existing today, and will continue to come in the future for the spiritual benefit of man. To suppose and accept that Spirituality has become the sole prerogative of any religion after the passing of the Master on those teachings it is based, and that sacred books are the only guide, shows the thoughtlessness of man.

How can we distinguish between a genuine and a false Master? There is in fact no such testing stone or magical formula except that of self-experience, for discriminating right from wrong, truth from falsehood, and reality from unreality. Even in the time of Emperor Janak (the father of Sita of the Ramayana) who was prepared to pay a big fee for the theoretical knowledge of this Science, only one, Yagyavalkya, out of all the Rishis, Yogis and Munis in India, was able to do so and won the prize. Yagyavalkya however had the moral courage to admit, "Gargi, I know the theory only but have no personal experience of it." On a second occasion, Emperor Janak proclaimed that he wanted a practical experience of this Science on a certain date, and that in a very short time too, not exceeding the time taken to straddle a horse and put each foot in its stirrup. Great Yogis and Rishis throughout the length and breadth of India were invited, but at the appointed time only one person stepped forward to accept the challenge. This was a hunchback named Ashtavakra, who had eight humps in his body. The audience, taking him for a maniac, laughed aloud at his appearance. Ashtavakra said, "How can you expect to get a spiritual experience from these cobblers you have collected, who have eyes only for the skin of the body but cannot see within?" The experience was duly given to the

Emperor within the allotted time. The point to consider is that at the time when Spirituality was thriving, only one person came forward to accept the challenge. In these times then, when materialism is on the increase, we do not find competent Masters growing like mushrooms. So search we must, not allowing false propaganda, the testimony of others, blind faith, the promise of future happiness, and our regard for position, wealth and pleasure to lead us astray. When such personalities come, they are competent to give life to millions of people who go to them. They are the children of Light, and give Light to all humanity.

Blind faith is one of the main obstacles to overcome. What we simply listen to, read, or follow without investigating as to what and where it will lead to, is blind faith. If one is careless and forgets the ends while following the means, so that he does not see whether he is nearing the end or not, it is still blind faith. When one goes to a Master and listens attentively to the explanations given by him on the subject of gaining Self-Knowledge by self-analysis, duly supported by one or more quotations from the valuable sayings of various Saints, he is intellectually convinced to tread the path as an experimental measure and act up to what the Master says with faith for the time being. This is the first stepping-stone to learn about Reality. When he has the first-hand experience, of whatever degree it may be, he is convinced and progresses from day to day. Today man listens to talks, lectures and sermons, accepts and believes these all his life, and takes for granted that he has been placed firmly on the way to salvation. But when death comes with all its sufferings, pangs of separation, and fears of the unknown, he realizes his mistake. Man's life-long habit of attachment to his body occupies all his thoughts, while friends, doctors, relatives and priests stand by helpless and despairing.

It is here that the Science of Para Vidya is of great help to us. The soul's withdrawal from the body is greatly eased and the

Master appears to receive and guide it further in the Beyond. Death is to such a one the happiest of events and like marriage, is the union with the Beloved. He has already visited and convinced himself of the superiority of the higher regions and traverses the familiar territory without fear. My Master, Hazur Baba Sawan Singh Ji, when impressing the need of spiritual practices on his disciples, used to say to them, "Go and see a disciple dying to become convinced." Saints believe in salvation during one's lifetime and not in salvation after death. This is indeed a simple and easy science, and the disciple should never rest content with his Initiation without spiritual experience. He should then devote regular time to the spiritual practices, and the Master must be regularly informed of his progress. He should constantly seek the guidance of his Master personally or by letter, without entertaining thoughts that he is bothering him. The Master knows by intuition how each disciple is faring and can remove most of his difficulties by thought transference or other means, but he wishes any difficulties in progress to be brought to his notice in writing.

The ancient path of Surat Shabd Yoga or Para Vidya is one that can be followed by men, women and children of all ages without any difficulty, unlike other ways which involve complicated strenuous exercises and control of the breath. These, at the most, lead to a slight control over the self and a few paltry powers. The latter methods also require a strong physique and a rich diet. As such, they are condemned by the Masters as unsuited to this age, and as involving physical dangers to the body.

The Science

In the physical body, two main currents are working that control life: one a motor current (breathing or prana) and the other a sensory current, which may also be called attention or surat. The Masters ignore the former so that the breathing is not interfered with and the life process goes on. The sensory current ramifies throughout the entire body, but its main center lies between and behind the two eyebrows, along with the mind. We have to withdraw the sensory current or spirit to its center.

Initiation

The mind will not allow man to have knowledge of the soul. Its nature is to see pleasure and its constant fluctuations are difficult to subdue. Attuning one's self with the internal Sound Current is the best way to calm the mind and practice concentration. It does not matter what school of thought or society a man may belong to. He has not to convert himself and can remain where he is. There are no hard and fast rules, no rituals, no ceremonies, no pomp and show, no offering of gifts, not even of flowers. All that a disciple has to do is to enter inside and henceforth consider the body as his laboratory. With regard to the theory, he has to understand the following, which is briefly the pith of what he will hear at Satsangs:

(1) The Master is not the body, he is the Power functioning through the body and uses it to teach and guide man in much the same way as a spirit uses a medium. Only in bodily form will the disciple be able to recognize his Master in the higher regions and here on earth.

(2) The Master is Shabd, Word, Nad, etc., all of which refer to the God-into-Expression Power of Light and Sound Principle. By having contact with this Power, man is led back to his true Home.

(3) For the sake of those who are disillusioned with life, and who yearn for permanent happiness and peace away from the world and its worries, the Word assumes a body to afford them solace. The Bible says, "Word was made flesh and

dwelt among us." Once a disciple contacts this Word (which is done at the time of Initiation by the Master), the audible form of this Word resides within him every moment of the day and night and never leaves him—not even after the end of man's physical existence on earth. It will go with him and stay with him until he achieves the final goal. The Word is also known as the Voice of God or the Sound Current, and is the Life impulse given by the Master at the time of Initiation. It may be heard as a sound coming from a distance and gradually develops into such sweetness that no music on earth can excel it. It is the Water of Life, the Spring of Immortality, the Elixir of Life, the Nectar of Spirituality, etc., that are spoken of in holy books.

(4) Man has an inner eye with which he can see within himself all the higher regions when the veil is rent asunder by a competent living Master. In this state he remains perfectly conscious and undergoes amazing experiences. To ascend into the higher regions without a competent Master is fraught with dangers.

Simran

The repetition of the holy names is given to the disciple at the time of Initiation as a guard against all dangers. It acts also as a password to all spiritual planes, gives strength and sustenance to the body and mind during trouble and afflictions, brings the soul nearer to the Master, is instrumental in achieving concentration, and imparts many other diverse powers. Simran taught by a so-called Master is just a bunch of words. But these very words become electrified when charged with the attention and grace of a real Master.

Initiation commences with the explanation and description of the inner spiritual regions and the way in which the path is to be pursued. The opening of the inner vision to see the inner regions, with their distinct heavenly lights, together with the contact with the Divine Link or Sound Current, constitutes the practical side of Initiation. Daily practice of these, combined with Simran, is meditation. In addition to this, the Master gives instructions on pure and simple living, the need of devoting regular time to the practices, and other words of sound advice. The whole ceremony takes from two to three hours. Diaries of one's spiritual progress must be kept and the mistakes of old and new disciples are corrected from time to time to insure progress.

Miracles

Master Saints never show any miracles to a disciple except in rare cases due to special circumstances. Miracles are in accordance with the laws of Nature but are nevertheless terrible entangling webs, detrimental to the highest ideals of man in his approach to Almighty God. It is a subject that an ordinary man would not care to study, for the simple reason that it requires immense self-control and training of the mind, with restrictions that he would not like to tolerate or pursue. The miraculous powers achieved after a lengthy period of time are instrumental in doing both good and harm, and as they are utilized more for harm than anything else, they are termed as a disease by all truly spiritual persons. The Masters are in possession of Supreme Power, but their mission is sacred. A disciple whose inner vision has been opened sees any number of miracles at each step. To hesitate to believe in a Master without seeing miracles is as foolish as a refusal to believe that a certain person is a multi-millionaire unless he shows us his money. He may have all his money deposited in a bank and wishes to spend it in the way that he chooses, without caring for public applause or approval. Out of an audience of several thousands watching a magician perform his tricks, only a very small number would thereby be induced to learn the art. Those who are anxious to see miracles are not true seekers.

General

Today the world is crying out for a better understanding, for peace and freedom from conflict. This science of self-analysis that reveals the Brotherhood of Man and the Fatherhood of God is the remedy which can reconstruct a healthy culture, and propagate harmony between man and man. He who claims to love the invisible God but has no regard or love for his visible fellow man is lost indeed. To love, revere and feel grateful to our fellow man is to love and revere God. So too, the love for the visible Master, our closest connecting link to God, is in reality love for the Supreme Father. We should therefore try to measure the depth of God's mercy and grace through a Master Saint, who is God's visible representative. It has Spirituality as its end and is not idolatry. The atmosphere in which such a genuine Master moves is charged with currents of peace and love which affect those who come into contact with him. Even letters written by or on behalf of him carry currents of ecstasy that influence the innermost recesses of the heart.

Guru precedes God. Such a person was Master Hazur Baba Sawan Singh Ji Maharaj, who remained with His disciples for a great number of years and now, even after He has left the body, still watches over His loved ones and also those who contacted Him once with love and sincerity in their hearts. Love knows no law, and He is still appearing in His Radiant Form, even on lower spiritual planes, for their sake. Not one, but hundreds can testify to what ignorant people would call an illusion. On the physical plane, He is still showering His blessings through His medium at Ruhani Satsang, Sawan Ashram, who now* in turn guides men in all spiritual matters. One bulb is fused and is replaced by another. The same Power works and the same Light now shines from a new bulb. All who approach the Master get positive experiences; and anybody who wishes to avail himself of such a golden opportunity has only to contact the Master and his wishes will be fulfilled, his heart will overflow with happiness, and his weary shoulders will be relieved of their burden of cares and worries.

*Here the words "His medium" and "now" pertain to the lifetime of Kirpal Singh Ji Maharaj at Sawan Ashram, ending August 21, 1974.

-Book Committee 1983

The original recording of this talk is available on CD and can be ordered by mail or via our website. Contact information is at the bottom of the last page.

BOOKS by Kirpal Singh

CROWN OF LIFE
A comparison of the various yogas and their scope; including Surat Shabd Yoga—the disciplined approach to Spirituality. Religious parallels and various modern movements cited. Paperback; 256 pages; index.

ISBN 978-0-942735-77-2

GODMAN
If there is always at least one authorized spiritual guide on earth at any time, what are the characteristics which will enable the honest seeker to distinguish him from those who are not competent? A complete study of the supreme mystics and their hallmarks. Paperback; 185 pages.

ISBN 978-0-942735-64-2

A GREAT SAINT: BABA JAIMAL SINGH
His Life and Teachings
A unique biography, tracing the development of one of the most outstanding Saints of modern times. Should be read by every seeker after God for the encouragement it offers. Also included, **A BRIEF LIFE SKETCH OF THE GREAT SAINT, BABA SAWAN SINGH,** the successor of Baba Jaimal Singh. He carried on Baba Ji's work, greatly expanding the Satsang and carrying it across the seas. Paperback; 230 pages; glossary; index.

ISBN 978-0-942735-27-7

THE JAP JI: The Message of Guru Nanak
An extensive explanation of the basic principles taught by Guru Nanak (1469-1539 A.D.) with comparative scriptures cited. Stanzas of the Hymns in English, as well as the original text in phonetic wording. Paperback; 189 pages; glossary.

ISBN 978-0-942735-81-9

HIS GRACE LIVES ON
During 17 days in the month of August 1974, preceding His physical departure on August 21st, Kirpal Singh gave 15 darshan talks, mostly in the form of questions and answers, to a small group of His disciples at His ashram in New Delhi, India. These talks have been bound together with the unabridged text from Master Kirpal's address to the Parliament of India and His 1971 afternoon darshan talk, True Meditation. Hard cover and paperback; 17 photos; 203 pages.

Hard cover ISBN 978-0-942735-93-2
Soft cover ISBN 978-0-9764548-3-0

THE LIGHT OF KIRPAL
A collection of 87 talks given from September 1969 to December 1971, containing extensive questions and answers between the Master and western disciples visiting at that time. Paperback; 446 pages; 15 photos.

ISBN 978-0-89142-033-0

MORNING TALKS

A transcription of a sequence of talks given by Sant Kirpal Singh between October 1967 and January 1969. The scope of the talks is broad covering many aspects of Spirituality in a direct and simple way, and, as such, the talks are intellectually enlightening. More importantly, the spirit of the talks reflects the pure and loving nature of the Speaker, whose life was a brilliant example of spirituality in action. Paperback; 258 pages.

ISBN 978-0-942735-16-1

NAAM or WORD

"In the beginning was the WORD... and the WORD was God." Quotations from Hindu, Buddhist, Islamic, and Christian sacred writings confirm the universality of this spiritual manifestation of God in religious tradition and mystical practices. Paperback; 335 pages. ISBN 978-0-942735-94-9

THE NIGHT IS A JUNGLE

A compendium of 14 talks delivered by the author prior to 1972, the first four of which were given in Philadelphia in 1955. The remaining ten talks were delivered in India. All of these talks were checked for their accuracy by Kirpal Singh prior to their compilation in this book. Paperback; 358 pages; with an introduction. ISBN 978-0-89142-017-0

PRAYER: Its Nature and Technique

Discusses all forms and aspects of prayer, from the most elementary to the ultimate state of "praying without ceasing." Also contains collected prayers from all religious traditions. Paperback; 147 pages; including appendix; index of references. ISBN 978-0-942735-50-5

SPIRITUALITY: What It Is

Explores the Science of Spirituality. Man has unravelled the mysteries of the starry welkin, sounded the depths of the seas, delved deep into the bowels of the earth, braved the blinding blizzards of snowy Mount Everest, and is now out exploring space so as to establish interplanetary relations, but sad to say, has not found out the mystery of the human soul within him. Paperback; 103 pages plus introductory. ISBN 978-0-942735-78-9

SPIRITUAL ELIXIR

Collected questions addressed to Kirpal Singh in private correspondence, together with respective answers. Also contains various messages given on special occasions. Paperback; 382 pages; glossary.

ISBN 978-0-942735-02-4

SURAT SHABD YOGA

The Yoga of the Celestial Sound Current. A perfect science, it is free from the drawbacks of other yogic forms. Emphasis is placed on the need for a competent living Master. Paperback, 74 pages.

ISBN 978-0-942735-95-6

THE TEACHINGS OF KIRPAL SINGH

Volume I: The Holy Path; 98 pages. ISBN 978-0-9764548-0-9

Volume II: Self Introspection/Meditation; 180 pages.

ISBN 978-0-9764548-1-6

Volume III: The New Life; 186 pages ISBN 978-0-9764548-2-3

Definitive statements from various talks and books by the author, collected to illuminate the aspects of self-discipline pertinent to Spirituality. Relevant questions are answered. Text selections are indexed to a source list at the end of each volume. This collection invites the reader to browse.

Three volumes sold as one book; 464 pages

THE WAY OF THE SAINTS

An encyclopedia of Sant Mat from every point of view. This is a collection of the late Master's short writings from 1949 to 1974. Included is a brief biography of Baba Sawan Singh, the author's Master, plus many pictures. Paperback; 418 pages. ISBN 978-0-89142-026-2

THE WHEEL OF LIFE & THE MYSTERY OF DEATH

Originally two separate books; now bound in one volume. The meaning of one's life on earth is carefully examined in the first text; in the following text, the reader is presented with the whys and wherefores of "the great final change called death." Paperback; 293 pages; plus index for the first text; and introduction. ISBN 978-0-942735-80-2

THE THIRD WORLD TOUR OF KIRPAL SINGH

This book was printed directly from the pages of Sat Sandesh magazine, the issues from October 1972 through February 1973, which were primarily devoted to Master Kirpal Singh's Third World Tour. 160 pages, 80 black and white pictures.

BOOKLETS BY KIRPAL SINGH

GOD POWER / CHRIST POWER / MASTER POWER
Discusses the ongoing manifestation of the Christ-Power and the temporal nature of the human bodies through which that Power addresses humanity. "Christ existed long before Jesus." Paperback; 17 pages.

HOW TO DEVELOP RECEPTIVITY
Three Circular Letters (of June 13, 1969; November 5, 1969; and January 27, 1970) concerning the attitudes which must be developed in order to become more spiritually receptive. Paperback; 20 pages.

MAN! KNOW THYSELF
A talk especially addressed to seekers after Truth. Gives a brief coverage of the essentials of Spirituality and the need for open-minded cautiousness on the part of the careful seeker. Paperback; 30 pages.

RUHANI SATSANG: Science of Spirituality
Briefly discusses "The Science of the Soul"; "The Practice of Spiritual Discipline"; "Death in life"; "The Quest for a True Master"; and "Surat Shabd Yoga." Paperback; 29 pages.

SEVEN PATHS TO PERFECTION
Describes the seven basic requisites enumerated in the prescribed self-introspective diary which aid immeasurably in covering the entire field of ethics, and help to invoke the Divine Mercy. Paperback; 20 pages.

SIMRAN: The Sweet Remembrance of God
Discusses the process of centering the attention within by repeating the "Original or Basic Names of God" given by a true Master. Paperback; 34 pages.

THE SPIRITUAL AND KARMIC ASPECTS OF THE VEGETARIAN DIET
An overview of the vegetarian diet containing a letter from Kirpal Singh on the Spiritual aspects, a letter from Sawan Singh on the karmic aspects, and excerpts from various books by Kirpal Singh. Paperback; 36 pages.

ISBN 978-0-942735-47-5

Books, Booklets and Audio-Visual Material of Master Kirpal Singh can be ordered from this new address or directly online.

RUHANI SATSANG®
250 "H" St. #50, Blaine, WA 98230-4033
1 (888) 530-1555   Fax (604) 530-9595 (Canada)
E-mail: MediaSales@RuhaniSatsangUSA.org
www.RuhaniSatsangUSA.org/mediasales.htm